BEING AN ACTIVE CITIZEN
OBEYING LAWS

by Vincent Alexander

po·go

Ideas for Parents and Teachers

Pogo Books let children practice reading informational text while introducing them to nonfiction features such as headings, labels, sidebars, maps, and diagrams, as well as a table of contents, glossary, and index.

Carefully leveled text with a strong photo match offers early fluent readers the support they need to succeed.

Before Reading

- "Walk" through the book and point out the various nonfiction features. Ask the student what purpose each feature serves.
- Look at the glossary together. Read and discuss the words.

Read the Book

- Have the child read the book independently.
- Invite him or her to list questions that arise from reading.

After Reading

- Discuss the child's questions. Talk about how he or she might find answers to those questions.
- Prompt the child to think more. Ask: What laws can you think of that you obey every day?

Pogo Books are published by Jump!
5357 Penn Avenue South
Minneapolis, MN 55419
www.jumplibrary.com

Library of Congress Cataloging-in-Publication Data

Names: Alexander, Vincent, author.
Title: Obeying laws / by Vincent Alexander.
Description: Minneapolis : Jump!, Inc., 2018.
Series: Being an active citizen | Includes index.
Identifiers: LCCN 2018009884 (print)
LCCN 2018008722 (ebook)
ISBN 9781641280242 (e-book)
ISBN 9781641280228 (hardcover : alk. paper)
ISBN 9781641280235 (pbk.)
Subjects: LCSH: Obedience (Law)—Juvenile literature.
Rule of law—Juvenile literature.
Classification: LCC K258 (print)
LCC K258 .A44 2018 (ebook)
DDC 340/.112—dc23
LC record available at https://lccn.loc.gov/2018009884

Editor: Kristine Spanier
Book Designer: Anna Peterson

Photo Credits: Odua Images/Shutterstock, cover; FangXiaNuo/Getty, 1; jgroup/iStock, 3 (left), 16 (bottom right); FocusDzign/Shutterstock, 3 (right); Danita Delimont/Getty, 4; kali9/Getty, 5; michael jung/iStock, 6-7; JBryson/iStock, 8-9; Michael Wheatley/Alamy, 10-11; Robert W. Kelley/Getty, 12; Bain News Service/Library of Congress, 13; White House Photo/Alamy, 14-15; Virunja/Shutterstock, 16 (left); MA8/Shutterstock, 16 (top right); inhauscreative/Getty, 17; Echo/Getty, 18-19; Steve Debenport/iStock, 20-21; gbh007/iStock, 23.

Printed in the United States of America at Corporate Graphics in North Mankato, Minnesota.

TABLE OF CONTENTS

CHAPTER 1

LAWS PROTECT US

Laws are rules the government makes. The government **enforces** them, too. We must **obey** laws. Why?

U.S. Capitol ·····▶

Laws protect us. They help keep peace and order. Obeying laws makes us active citizens.

How do laws protect us? We must wear seat belts. Children can't have dangerous jobs. Factories can't dump waste into lakes.

seat belt

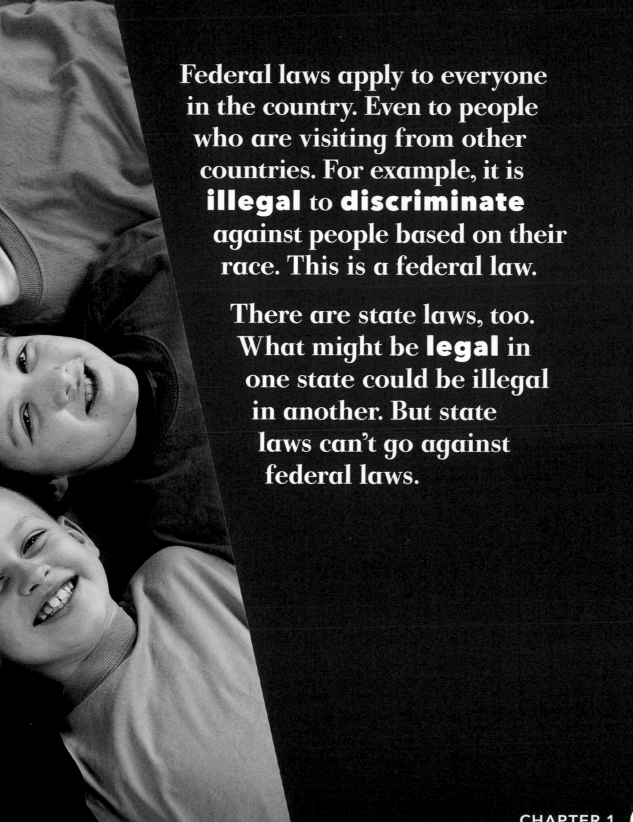

Federal laws apply to everyone in the country. Even to people who are visiting from other countries. For example, it is **illegal** to **discriminate** against people based on their race. This is a federal law.

There are state laws, too. What might be **legal** in one state could be illegal in another. But state laws can't go against federal laws.

TAKE A LOOK!

Laws about the same thing can be different from state to state. An example is motorcycle helmet laws. What is the law where you live?

- ■ = no law
- ■ = people under age 18 must wear a motorcycle helmet
- ■ = people under age 19 must wear a motorcycle helmet
- ■ = people under 21 must wear a motorcycle helmet
- ■ = everyone must wear a motorcycle helmet

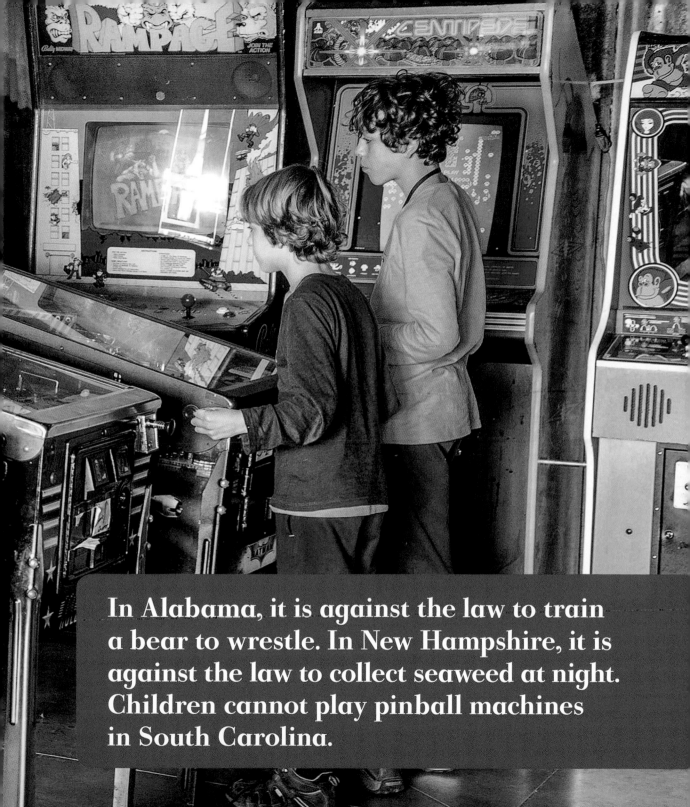

In Alabama, it is against the law to train a bear to wrestle. In New Hampshire, it is against the law to collect seaweed at night. Children cannot play pinball machines in South Carolina.

CHAPTER 2

OUR RIGHTS

Do laws only ban behaviors? No. Laws also protect our rights. These include the freedom of speech. Freedom of religion. Freedom of the **press**. Another is the right to **protest**. Dr. Martin Luther King, Jr. marched in the 1960s. For what? **Civil rights**.

Dr. Martin Luther King, Jr.

In the early 1900s, women marched for the right to vote. These protests helped change laws.

As our **values** change, our laws change. How? Lawmakers learn what is important to us. A bill is introduced to Congress. It is voted on. If it passes, the bill goes to the president. The president can sign it into a new law.

WHAT DO YOU THINK?

Our rights include the right to "life, **liberty**, and the pursuit of happiness." How do you think our laws make that happen?

President Trump

law

CHAPTER 3

· ·

ENFORCING AND OBEYING

Laws only work if we enforce them. How are laws enforced?

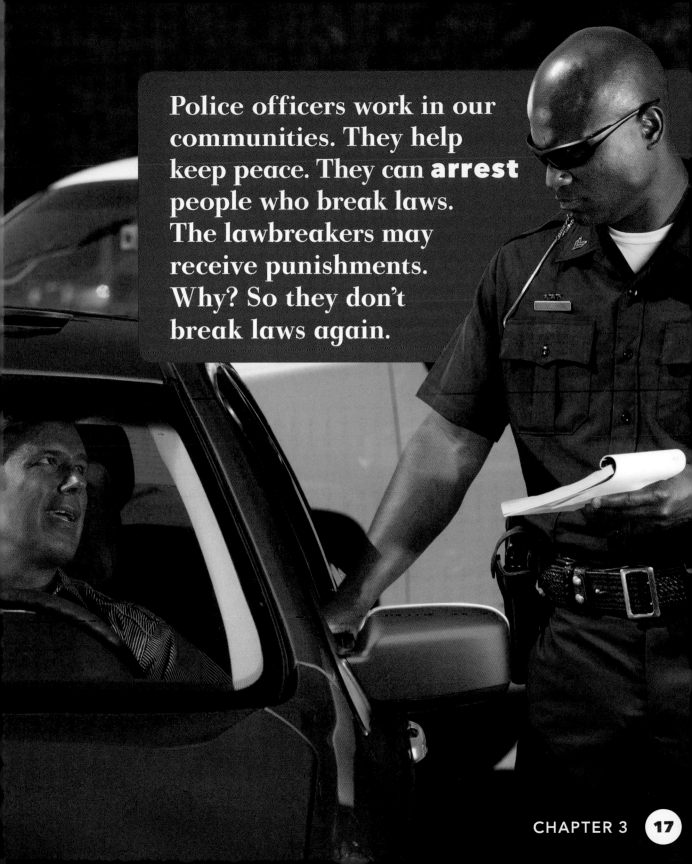

Police officers work in our communities. They help keep peace. They can **arrest** people who break laws. The lawbreakers may receive punishments. Why? So they don't break laws again.

leash

Think about the laws you follow every day. Do you keep your dog on a leash during walks? Do you use crosswalks to cross the street? Do you put your garbage into trash cans?

WHAT DO YOU THINK?

Laws are similar to rules at school. What happens to students who don't obey the rules? How is this similar to people who don't obey laws?

Active citizens work to improve the lives of others. Obeying laws helps. It makes our communities better places to live. By obeying laws, we help promote peace.

ACTIVITIES & TOOLS

WRITE A LETTER TO A NEWSPAPER EDITOR

In Chapter 1 of this book, unusual state laws are mentioned. Does your state have any outdated laws? Do some research to find out. Is there a law that you think should be changed? What is it? When was it put into place? Why did lawmakers feel it was necessary? Is it still enforced?

Write a letter to your local newspaper. Explain what the law is and what you think should be done about it. Opening a public discussion is one way to get the attention of lawmakers.

Your letter should:
- identify yourself, including your full name and grade
- state your purpose
- express your feelings
- thank the editor for his or her time
- include your signature

Make sure to also include:
- your address (this will not be printed in the newspaper)
- phone number (so the editor can verify you wrote the letter; this will not be printed in the newspaper)
- date you wrote your letter
- name of editor and newspaper

GLOSSARY

arrest: To stop and hold someone by the power of law.

civil rights: The individual rights that all members of a democratic society have to freedom and equal treatment under the law.

Congress: The lawmaking body of the United States made up of the Senate and the House of Representatives.

discriminate: To treat someone unfairly while someone else is treated better.

enforces: Makes sure that a law or rule is obeyed.

illegal: Against the law.

legal: Of or having to do with the law.

liberty: Freedom.

obey: To carry out or to follow orders or instructions.

press: The journalists and the organizations that collect, publish, and broadcast the news.

protest: To make a demonstration or statement against something.

values: Principles of behavior and beliefs about what is important in life.

INDEX

TO LEARN MORE

Learning more is as easy as 1, 2, 3.

1) Go to www.factsurfer.com

2) Enter "obeyinglaws" into the search box.

3) Click the "Surf" button to see a list of websites.

With factsurfer, finding more information is just a click away.